PIRATES
STICKER BOOK

Ahoy there shipmate, welcome aboard!
This book belongs to

Pirate ....

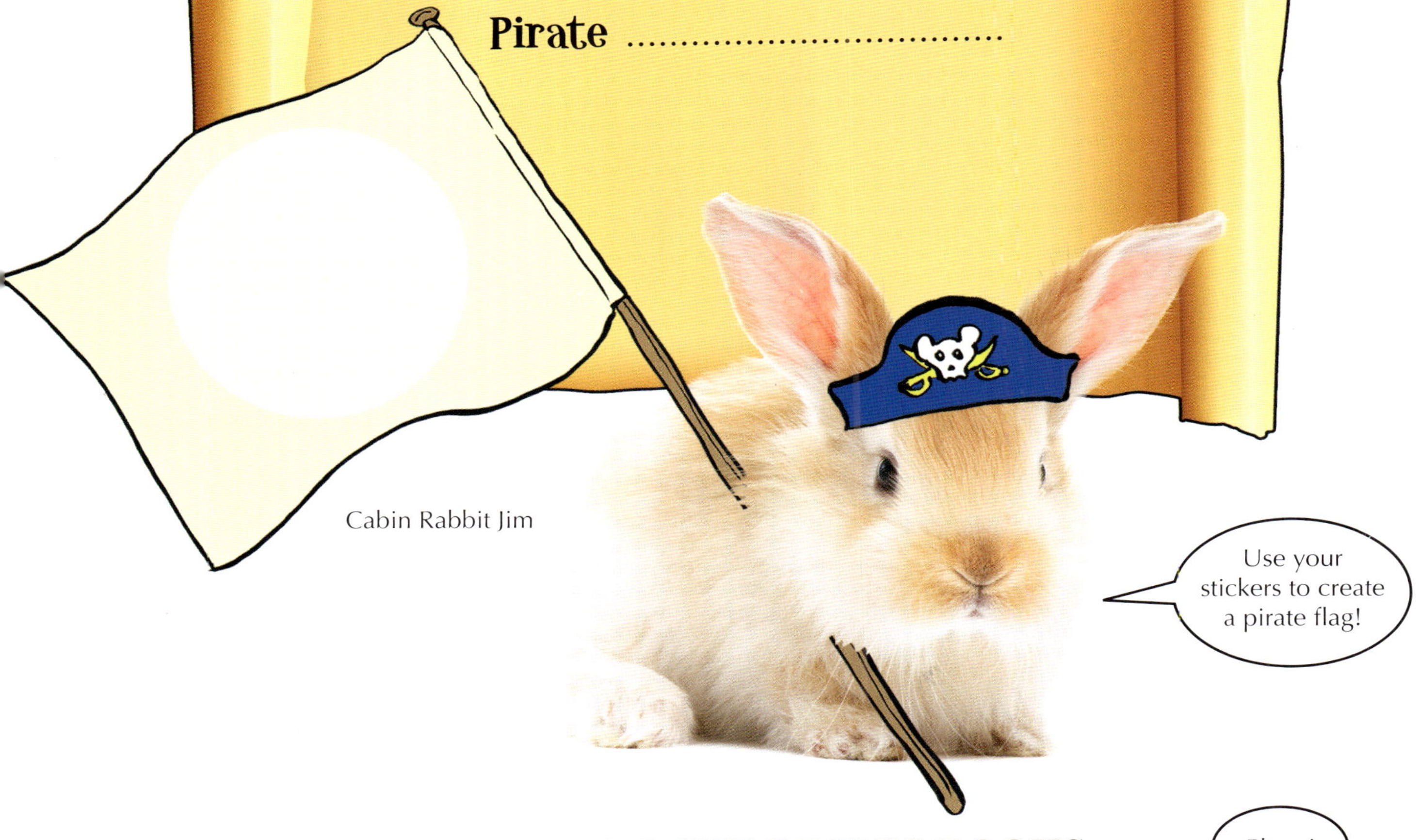

Cabin Rabbit Jim

Use your stickers to create a pirate flag!

MACMILLAN CHILDREN'S BOOKS

No animals were harmed during the creation of this book

Oooh Aaarrrgh, Me Hearties

Come and meet the dastardly crew!

Seasick Puppies!

The kitchen crew are feeling queasy.

Give every puppy a bucket, before Seaman Squawk has to swab the decks!

Pirate Breakfast

Look lively, you lazy lot! It's time for a hearty pirate breakfast.

Star Paws Stickers Start Here!

Eye patch!

Use these to create a pirate flag

Oooh Arrrrr, Me Hearties

Earrings!

A belt for Best Mate

Hats for the three chicks!

How about a moustache? There are loads to choose from!

Oooh Aaarrrgh, Me Hearties
Armbands anyone?
Hidden Treasure!
Hats for the chicks

Hidden Treasure!

Use these stickers to create your treasure map!

Shiver Me Timbers!

Shiver Me Timbers!
Use these to dress Larry Lookout and Blinky M. Mole.
For Mouse.
Seasick Puppies!
Hats and buckets for the seasick kitchen crew.
More eye patches!
I ♥ SEA
Pirate Breakfast
Choose what the pirates will eat – and wear!
A bib for a messy bunny?

Pirate Breakfast
Don't forget the eye patch!
Try these on G. P. Ginger
Scoundrels and Scallywags!
For Tiddles McNasty

Scoundrels and Scallywags!
Outfits for Loose-cannon Chris
Some of these should help them float!
Perils of the Sea!
Use these on the weather-beaten pirates
Shipwreck!
For Scuba Mole
For Scuba Cat

Shipwreck!

Use these stickers to fill the shipwreck scene

Bunny in a Barrel

Outfits for Private Thumper (you'll be spoilt for choice)

Pirate earrings!

Pirate Bling!
Gold for Cut-throat Clive
Gold bracelets anyone?
Rock-a-bye Pirates
Hats, pyjamas and blankets for the animals!
Do these belong
to Snuffles?

Use your stickers to help everyone wake up with a big pirate feast.

Scoundrels and Scallywags!

Walk the plank, you yellow-bellied, lily-livered scurvy dogs!

Perils of the Sea!

These weather-beaten pirates have seen some fierce battles – just look at the state they're in!

Use your stickers to add peg-legs, hooks and eye patches.

Peg Leg Paul

Eric the Gunner

Hammy

Shipwreck!

Hooray, what a cracking bounty!
Come on lads, get those snorkels and flippers on,
it's time to dive into the deep . . .

Use your stickers
to complete this
underwater scene.

Bunny in a Barrel

It's a hot day and Private Thumper is cooling off in a water barrel. Come on Thumper, get out of there and on with some work!

Use your stickers to find him a shady pirate hat and an eye patch too.

Pirate Bling!

Cut-throat Clive has plundered treasure from a rival galleon.

Use your stickers to cover Clive in pirate treasure.

Rock-a-bye Pirates

Shhh . . . It's been a long day and the crew are settling down to sleep in their hammocks.

Use your stickers to get them ready for bed. Tuck them in and wish them all good night.